Read All About CATS

SIAMESE CATS

LYNN M. STONE

The Rourke Corporation, Inc.
Vero Beach, Florida 32964

PHOTO CREDITS
© Chris Luneski: cover, pages 6, 9, 10, 13, 16, 22;
© Norvia Behling: pages 4, 7, 12, 15, 18, 19, 21

CREATIVE SERVICES:
East Coast Studios, Merritt Island, Florida

EDITORIAL SERVICES:
Janice L. Smith for Penworthy Learning Systems

Library of Congress Cataloging-in-Publication Data

Stone, Lynn M.
    Siamese cats / by Lynn M. Stone.
        p. cm. — (Cats)
    Includes bibliographical references (p. 24) and index.
    Summary: Provides an introduction to the history, physical
characteristics, habits, and breeding of Siamese cats.
        ISBN 0-86593-555-6
    1. Siamese cat Juvenile literature. [1. Siamese cat. 2. Cats.] I. Title.
II. Series: Stone, Lynn M.- Cats.
SF449.S5S76 1999
636.8'25—dc21
                                                                99-30639
                                                                    CIP

Printed in the USA

TABLE OF CONTENTS

SIAMESE CATS

Perhaps no type of cat is better known than the Siamese. This cat's unusual behavior and looks set it apart from other **breeds** (BREEDZ), or kinds, of cats.

The Siamese is an Asian breed. Like other Asian and African breeds, the Siamese has a long, slender, graceful body. But many Siamese, especially in North America, are extra slender.

Many modern Siamese have narrow, wedge-shaped faces. This Siamese wears the classic seal point coat, named for the dark (seal) points— face, feet, ears, tail—of the cat.

The early Siamese cats shown in England and North America had crossed eyes and **kinked** (KINGKT), or bent, tails. That curious look was desired—or even required—for the cat to be shown and judged against other Siamese in cat shows.

This snowshoe Siamese has the blue eyes typical of the breed. But this cat also shows a fuller face and body than many North American Siamese.

Siamese and other cats see things in some colors—blues, greens, and yellows—but they don't seem able to pick out reds.

Some time ago, however, Siamese cat breeders decided that it wasn't really desirable for the cats to have crossed eyes and kinked tails. They began breeding only Siamese cats that did not have crossed eyes and kinked tails. Now, nearly all Siamese cats have normal eyes and tails.

CAT BREEDS

Most house cats are mixed breeds. Their recent **ancestors** (AN SESS terz) have not been any one type of cat. Mixed breed cats may be part Persian or part Siamese or part any other breed. But they are not of any *one* breed.

The Siamese, however, is a true cat breed. A female Siamese and a male Siamese will produce offspring that strongly resemble the parents. The kittens will have the color, shape, voice, and fur of Siamese cats.

Siamese cats come in many different color patterns. The color of a cat's coat doesn't usually tell to which breed it belongs, however. This kitten is a blue point Siamese.

People create breeds of animals over a long period of time by choosing the mother and father animals. There are, for example, about 80 breeds of cats.

By carefully selecting which Siamese cats to mate, cat breeders have made changes even within the breed. Siamese cats were generally heavier than they are today. By picking the most slender Siamese as parents, breeders have made the Siamese a slender breed.

Some Siamese breeders are bringing back the full-faced Siamese cats of years past. This is a lynx point Siamese.

WHAT A SIAMESE CAT LOOKS LIKE

The modern "Siamese look" does not appeal to all Siamese cat lovers. The breed's popularity has declined since reaching a peak in the 1950s. The reason, many believe, is the super-thin look of many modern Siamese cats.

The Siamese is a pointed breed. Although the color of the points may vary, all Siamese cats have darker points than bodies.

The Siamese, like other breeds from warm countries, is an active cat. But this lynx point Siamese kitten has taken a time-out.

Some breeders are working to bring back the Siamese with the "apple head" look (see cover). These cats have fuller faces and heavier bodies than the new-look Siamese.

The original Siamese was a cat with a light, almost white, body, and dark points—face, ears, feet, and tail. The point colors, which were a rich dark brown, became known as "seal."

The seal point Siamese is still a popular color, but it's not the only Siamese color. The cream tabby point, for example, has points only slightly darker than the body.

The Siamese has bright blue eyes and a long, narrow head that is almost heart-shaped.

A Siamese has long ears that are wide at the base. Its legs are long and slim even though the first Siamese were apparently short-legged.

Siamese cats weigh from 6 to 12 pounds (2.5-5.5 kilograms).

Here a Siamese shows the deep blue eyes and seal points of the breed's best known color pattern. A cat's whiskers are very sensitive and help it find its way around, especially in low light.

THE HISTORY OF SIAMESE CATS

The Siamese breed began in Asia more than 500 years ago. A scientist from Europe saw cats with white bodies and dark points in central Asia. Meanwhile, similar cats were known in Siam, which is called Thailand today.

No one knows for sure just who owned the dark-pointed cats in Thailand. The **legend** (LEJ end), however, is that the Siamese was a breed owned by Buddhist **monks** (MUNKS) and Siam's kings, queens, and nobles. The cat is still sometimes called the palace cat or the royal cat of Siam.

The range of Siamese colors has been increased by breeders over the years. Changing colors, however, hasn't changed the Siamese's love of cat chat.

17

In truth, Siamese cats may have lived in the homes of Siamese people, too. No one has ever proved that the cats lived only in temples and palaces. They certainly would have been helpful as mouse and rat killers throughout all Siam.

The beginnings of the Siamese breed are not clear. It is certain, however, that the lilac point color pattern, shown here, did not exist originally.

These Siamese kittens are far removed from their ancestor—the small African wildcat.

In the 1880s a few Siamese cats were brought to England. Their unusual looks and lively personality made them a favorite of cat lovers. By 1900 a few of the cats had been sold to wealthy Americans for $1,000 each. That makes those British-born cats among the most expensive cats ever.

OWNING A SIAMESE

Siamese cats are still good mousers. That's because they're very active, **agile** (AJ ul) pets. They move quickly, often, and smoothly.

Many people want a cat to talk to. But not everyone wants a cat that talks back. Siamese are the most "talkative" of cats. Some people love cat chat. Others prefer a quiet breed.

Almost like dogs, Siamese cats are quite demanding of their human masters. They love attention. One thing—a Siamese will never be ignored.

Mischief comes naturally to a Siamese cat. Without a tree, this kitten will settle for a climb up the curtain.

GLOSSARY

agile (AJ ul) — able to move the body easily, quickly, and with great skill

ancestor (AN SESS ter) — those in the past from whom a person or animal has descended; direct relatives prior to one's grandparents

breed (BREED) — a particular group of domestic animals having several of the same characteristics; a kind of domestic animal within a group of many kinds, such as a *Bengal* cat or a *Persian* cat

kinked (KINGKT) — having a sharp bend or crease

legend (LEJ end) — a fictional story that has been told often, usually to explain a natural event

monk (MUNK) — a man who is a member of a religious group and lives in a temple or monastery

A red lynx point Siamese kitten shows none of the dark points of the original Siamese. Breeders have learned to change or add color patterns within many cat breeds.

INDEX

FURTHER READING

Find out more about Siamese cats and cats in general with these helpful books and information sites:

• Clutton-Brock, Juliet. *Cat.* Knopf, 1997
• Editors of Owl Magazine. *The Kids' Cat Book.* Greey de Pencier, 1990
• Evans, Mark. *ASPCA Pet Care Guide for Kids/Kittens.* Dorling Kindersley, 1992
• Scott, Carey. *Kittens.* Dorling Kindersley, 1992
• National Siamese Cat Club, 5865 Hillandale Drive, Nashport, OH 43830
• Siamese Cat Society of America, 304 S.W. 13th St., Ft. Lauderdale, FL 33315
• Cat Fanciers' Association on line @ www.cfainc.org